There's nothing complicated or taxing. If you stick to the basic principles set out here, your language skills and confidence will grow... and that feels really good.
David McGowan, Student of Spanish

This book is wonderfully concise, but don't think it lacks depth! Each chapter prompts you to think: what are your goals in learning Spanish; what motivates you to learn; how do you like to learn? When you understand yourself, you can start learning or improving your Spanish. Highly recommended.
Cath Alderson, President, Club Hispánico de Hillingdon

This is a really accessible book that provides students with a range of language learning strategies that are easy to implement. Although María Blanco focuses on Spanish, the principles that she provides are equally applicable to other languages. A great help to language learners!
Kate Weir, Principal Lecturer, University of Westminster

This is a little book that is of great value, not only for those who are learning Spanish, but also for their teachers. I wish I had had this guide when I was teaching in Adult Education years ago!
Yolanda Belle Isle, Retired Teacher of Spanish

Packed with brilliant practical tips, such as: how to memorise effectively for the long term, how to get clear on which areas you need more support, and the importance of finding a teacher who is not only well trained but passionate. Buy the book, you'll save yourself a lot of time whilst enjoying focus and freedom as you learn.
Belinda Ray, Creator and Teacher, Wild About Spanish

HOW TO LEARN SPANISH

HOW TO LEARN SPANISH

A guide to powerful principles and strategies for
successful learning and self-empowerment

María Blanco

HIKARI
PRESS

Contents

Introduction

Welcome to *How to Learn Spanish*, a guide to powerful principles and strategies for language learners who would like to:

- speed up their progress in speaking, listening, reading and writing
- make the process of learning more playful and creative
- feel empowered and self-confident as language learners
- take charge of their learning experience

The idea for this book came while I was teaching Spanish as a foreign language to groups of adults on England's south coast many years ago. The students were very motivated and participated actively in class, but many of them had little experience of learning a language at school. They lacked confidence, and from time to time they would ask for advice on how to work on their pronunciation and grammar when studying at home. It soon became clear to me that students were happily taking on board my language learning tips.

I had similar experiences when teaching in schools, universities, and privately. I came to the conclusion that, just as I myself had observed when learning foreign languages at school, the majority of my students had never been taught strategies for learning foreign languages effectively.

After taking an MA in Modern Languages in Education, I started regularly training my students of Spanish in language learning strategies. This time I did not wait for them to ask me for tips. My training sessions were short and simple but, to my delight, student feedback was excellent. I noticed many improvements: students were learning faster, getting higher marks in exams, speaking better and with more confidence, memorising vocabulary more easily, enjoying the process of studying more, and gaining more self-confidence. The positive effects of the training were crystal clear.

Now, after twenty years of teaching strategies for vocabulary, pronunciation, grammar and language skills, and seeing excellent results, I have no doubt: the application of the principles that you are about to discover can transform your language learning experience for the better.

How to Learn Spanish is the revised edition of my first book, *Smart Ways for Learning Spanish*. The main changes are the addition of a 'What about you?' section at the end of each chapter to prompt self-reflection questions, as well as illustrations which will help you to remember the principles and strategies more easily and make reading more fun. Answering the questions will give you clarity about your current learning and suggest simple changes to make your learning more productive and enjoyable. So, let's get started!

THE STARTING POINT

Chapter 1
What motivates you?

Daniel had a strong motivation for learning Spanish. He was a busy professional who had just bought a house in a small village in the mountains of Spain. He had fallen in love with the village, got on very well with the neighbours, and was planning to spend long holiday periods there. He was a very social person, but there was only one problem: his neighbours hardly spoke any English and Daniel's Spanish was almost non-existent.

When he enrolled in the Spanish course, he was a bit worried. 'I am not good at foreign languages. I struggled a lot at school. I could hardly put a sentence together in French!'

Daniel was turning up early to every class, paying a lot of attention, and doing his best in the class activities; despite this, a few weeks into the course, he started to struggle to keep up with the pace of the lessons, particularly with the grammar explanations and speaking activities. One day, after the lesson, he told me that he felt that everyone else in the class seemed to be doing better than him. I encouraged him to be more positive about his own progress, which was real and undoubtedly happening. I also reminded him of his motivation: that Spanish would give him the opportunity to enjoy more social life in the village. 'Yes, that is the most important thing for me, really,' he said. 'That is why I am taking this course.'

Fortunately, a few weeks later, he had to travel to Spain to oversee renovation work being done on his house. When he came back, he was transformed. I could see him taking part in the group speaking activities with a confidence and ease that I had never seen in him before.

'How was your trip?' I asked him.

'Great!' he replied. 'I went to the grocery shop and to restaurants and managed to order almost everything in Spanish. I even introduced myself and had a little chat with people I met at one of the parties I was invited to.'

Daniel sailed through the rest of the course, continuing to make progress and build self-confidence. It was a pleasure to see the change.

Daniel's story is similar to that of many students I have taught: clear motivation for learning Spanish keeps them doing the necessary work. As they keep at it, they overcome the challenges that inevitably come up in grammar, speaking, listening, vocabulary, and so on. As they start seeing good progress, they feel more confident, and as a result, they enjoy the process of learning more. It creates a success cycle, and motivation is the driving force.

What about you?

Taking the time to define what motivates you to learn Spanish will be invaluable on your learning journey. Pause for a moment to answer the question. Clarity about your motivation will help you activate the inner and outer resources you need to make good progress.

Why do you choose to learn Spanish?

	√
To travel to Spanish-speaking countries	
To move to and live in Spanish-speaking countries	
To be more integrated in the Spanish-speaking country where I already live	
To connect more with people from Spanish-speaking countries	
To use Spanish in my job	
To explore Hispanic culture (cinema, literature, art) in more depth	
I love the way the Spanish language sounds	
I love learning languages	
To develop a new skill	
To learn something new	

Do you have other reasons for learning Spanish?

Chapter 2
How do good language learners learn?

I met Susie on the first day of a coaching course in Madrid. It was obvious she was keen to practise her basic Spanish with me and other native speakers attending the course. On one occasion, she was struggling to tell me something in Spanish and I asked whether she would prefer us to switch to English. She responded without hesitation, 'No, gracias. Prefiero hablar español. Necesito practicar.' (No, thank you. I prefer to speak in Spanish. I need to practise.)

As the days went by, I became more impressed with Susie's determination and her skilful way of communicating in Spanish with such a small repertoire of vocabulary. I asked her if she had taken a Spanish course.

'Well, I've studied mostly by myself, with the help of online materials,' she said. 'I love taking language courses, although I haven't managed to do a Spanish one yet. To be honest, I just couldn't fit one in at the moment. I'm busy managing new projects at work and my family life is hectic. Instead, I'm studying by myself, at my own pace, using Spanish online materials.'

I was surprised. 'Is that the only formal studying you've done?'

'Yes! And our chat on the first day we met was my first attempt at having a conversation with a native Spanish speaker.'

Susie and I got on well and spent a lot of time together during that week. I could see her moving around and taking full advantage of opportunities to mingle with Spanish speakers. On sightseeing tours, she joined the Spanish guide instead of the English one, checking her dictionary and asking some of us for translations. She was determined, but also playful and patient with herself. It was fascinating to see how she was making the most of the situation to immerse herself in the language. Susie's proactive approach to learning left me in no doubt that she would easily achieve her goal to be a competent Spanish speaker.

What makes some people, like Susie, do so well at learning a foreign language? As I became more interested in this question, I began to pay more attention to the attitudes and skills of my best students. I also read studies that investigated the strategies used by good and not-so-good language learners.

I concluded that good language learners:

- Use a wide variety of language learning strategies
- Are skilful with self-management strategies like planning, checking progress, problem solving, and self-assessment

Research has also found that good language learners:

- Maintain a good level of motivation because they usually have many reasons to learn
- Take an active approach to learning
- Use strategies suitable for their individual needs and adapt to different learning environments
- Pay attention to both the meaning and form of words
- Actively seek opportunities to practise the language in real-life situations

Perhaps one final attribute that is relevant to all good language learners is their ability to maintain focus when learning. They can 'hold the reins' of their attention while learning, and that is a powerful advantage.

What about you?

What works well for you when learning Spanish or another foreign language? Bring to mind any simple strategies you have used, even simple ones like writing down a word several times. It is useful and empowering to become aware of what we have already discovered that works well.

The strategies that have worked well for me are:

Chapter 3
What are your Spanish learning goals?

Clarifying and writing down your goals can be very helpful for making your learning more effective and enjoyable. These are goals that will:

- Help to make your destination clear
- Assist you in selecting learning strategies
- Guide you in assessing your progress

It is easier to keep the momentum going if you are excited about the destination. That is why it is essential to have goals that you feel enthusiastic about and that inspire you to keep moving forward.

The most effective goals are:

- Connected to a broader life vision or dream, like wanting to connect more with Spanish-speaking friends or relatives, wanting to live in a Spanish-speaking country, or working for an international company that services Spanish-speaking customers. When you connect your goals with a broader vision, you are likely to be more willing to commit the time and resources needed.

- Ambitious yet grounded. Goals should take you beyond your comfort zone, and at the same time you should feel they are achievable. It is a challenging balance, but it is possible.

Goal-setting can also be enhanced by:

- Starting the goals with action words such as 'increase', 'maintain', 'correct', 'complete'.

- Using your imagination and senses to feel and see the future you want to experience. Where do you see yourself communicating in Spanish? What are you saying and doing? Who is interacting with you? What can you hear? What are you feeling?

- Asking for professional help. The guidance of a good language teacher or coach can take you far; good professionals have a lot of experience with the mechanics of success.

Setting goals for learning a foreign language may be a new experience for you. Most people are not taught to think and take decisions about what they want to achieve in their school years, but it is an empowering exercise. I highly recommend that you think about your goals and write them down.

What about you?

Are you already clear about your Spanish learning goals? If you are, write them down, read them out loud, and see whether they resonate with what you really want. Check whether they connect with your broader life vision, and whether they are ambitious and yet realistic for you. If you are not clear, and are in need of inspiration, I suggest you read the examples below.

My Spanish learning goals are:

Communication goals

- To get by in Spanish: greet friends and say goodbye, order food and drinks, go shopping, and make travel arrangements
- To discuss current affairs with native speakers
- To understand the news on TV and in newspapers without constantly having to resort to a dictionary
- To negotiate a business contract
- To discuss films and books more fluently

Proficiency goals

- To achieve a 'get by' / intermediate / advanced level
- To maintain my current level of Spanish
- To get an international certificate in Spanish as a Foreign Language such as DELE or SIELE

Practice goals

- To design flashcards with vocabulary from topics covered in my Spanish lessons
- To learn specific vocabulary for writing emails and dealing with phone calls
- To get into the habit of checking the meaning and listening to and repeating the pronunciation of words I want to learn
- To correct some of the frequent errors I make in pronunciation
- To memorise verb endings of the present / past / future tense
- To spend 30 minutes, four days a week, working through my self-study materials

Be open and flexible about the ways in which you work towards your learning goals, because life situations tend to keep changing! You may start your Spanish course, and suddenly find yourself going through a change of job or relationship and having little time for self-study. The opposite may also be true. You may be moving from a full-time to a part-time job and find that you have more free time to finally embark on the Spanish course you have been waiting to take for some time.

In my view, the best way to make the most of your learning experience despite changes of circumstance is to learn how to use a number of different language learning strategies and to adapt to different learning environments. And this is what *How to Learn Spanish* is about: it teaches you a wide range of strategies so that you can select strategies suitable for your learning preferences and lifestyle. It also teaches you powerful principles that make learning time both efficient and enjoyable. So, let's start with the principles.

POWERFUL PRINCIPLES

Chapter 4
Taking Two Complementary Approaches

There are two complementary approaches to learning a foreign language.

The first is the classic, formal approach that you may have experienced at school. It involves activities like a Spanish language course with a private tutor or coach; practising vocabulary, pronunciation, and grammar with educational resources; and scheduling self-study time.

The second approach is informal. It involves immersing yourself in environments where you get to use Spanish as 'naturally' as possible without thinking too much about how the language works. Popular informal learning activities are things like listening to Spanish music, watching movies, playing computer games, and interacting with native speakers through social media or face-to-face social events.

The combination of the two approaches, formal and informal, is powerful because each one fulfils different needs. The formal approach helps you to understand how the language works and to communicate correctly. And the informal approach helps you to become fluent, to engage your emotions, and to make a deeper connection with the people and culture of Spanish-speaking countries.

The combination of both approaches produces the best results in language learning, making it a powerful principle.

What about you?

How have you learnt foreign languages
so far?

	√
I have enrolled in classes or had private tuition	
I have used flashcards	
I have kept a vocabulary notebook	
I have taken exams	
I have completed vocabulary and grammar exercises from textbooks or online resources	
I have listened to music	
I have watched films	
I have read books	
I have attended dancing lessons	
I have looked for opportunities to meet with native speakers	
I have used the language on social media	
I have gone on holiday to countries where I could practise	

Chapter 5
Reading and Listening

I was surprised by Alice's request when she approached me during her first advanced level Spanish class.

'Could I please have a reading list of Spanish books?'

'Yes. There's a list available on our website. What kind of books do you like reading?'

'All sorts, but mainly science fiction, stories of intrigue. Anything with a good plot.'

'Have you read any Spanish books so far?'

'I haven't, but I sometimes read newspapers and magazines. I'd like to try books now.'

What surprised me about Alice's request was her being so proactive. She had not even waited until the end of the first class. I had never had a request like this before.

Alice's spoken Spanish was not particularly good at the start of the course, considering that she had studied Spanish for several years at school. Many other students in the class spoke more fluently and had more sophisticated vocabulary. But about three months later, I noticed Alice's language skills were getting significantly better with each class, and by the end of the year she was one of the best in the group.

In the final exam, Alice's oral presentation was by far the best in the class, and the best I had seen for many years at her level. She used specialist vocabulary very well, her grammar was refined, and there was confidence and poise in her delivery. Her classmates went quiet and listened to her presentation with much attention. We were all impressed.

A couple of days later, before travelling back to her hometown for the holiday, she came to my office to say goodbye.

'Thanks for the classes, Maria. I very much enjoyed your lessons.'

'I'm glad. I enjoyed teaching you too. It was a pleasure to see you making so much progress during the year and to see your outstanding presentation. How did you do it?'

'Well, reading a lot in Spanish made a big difference. Apart from the usual newspapers, I managed to read four books on the course reading list – books by Isabel Allende and Manuel Vazquez Montalbán. I loved the novels and got more confident when I realised that I could understand a lot more than I expected. It felt great. I also watched a few Almodóvar films with my housemate, who is also studying Spanish. We used subtitles because some of the characters speak very fast, but I enjoy Almodóvar's films very much. And the more I watch, the easier it gets.'

Alice's story reveals another powerful principle: reading and listening regularly to Spanish which is interesting and understandable helps you to learn with more ease. If the content is interesting and you can understand most of it, you get moire motivated to keep reading and listening, and you pay more attention to the language. The more attention you pay and the more you understand, the more language 'sticks' in your memory. The more language sticks in your memory, the more it expands your ability to understand and express yourself in Spanish. It is a virtuous circle of success, just as it was for Alice.

What about you?

Are you reading and listening regularly to Spanish materials that you find interesting and understandable?

	√
Graded readers	
Spanish films	
Spanish songs	
Spanish podcasts	
Spanish radio stations	
Other materials	

Tips for selecting reading and listening materials:

- Readers that include glossaries of vocabulary and audio versions of the stories are especially helpful.

- Choose films you are genuinely interested in. If necessary, make the language understandable by using subtitles.

- Music awakens our emotions and helps us to memorise vocabulary. Go for songs that you really enjoy. It is easy to find the lyrics and translations online.

Chapter 6
Focusing on the key ingredients

Julia was looking upset after her Spanish oral exam. 'My speaking isn't good,' she said before leaving the classroom. With the next student to be examined already waiting at the door, I was unable to take the time to speak with her. But I kept thinking about Julia's comment.

Her pronunciation was excellent, probably one of the best in the class, and her range of vocabulary was good. The weak points in her speaking were grammar and fluency. She was slow and hesitant, and made mistakes when using verbs and sentences with noun and adjective agreements.

I have seen many cases like Julia: the lack of good grammar skills slows down the student's fluency, self-doubt kicks in, and they conclude that they are not good at speaking. But, as in Julia's case, their conclusion is an overgeneralisation. The problem is not their speaking skill as a whole. The weakness, and what needs to be improved, is often one of the key ingredients of the spoken language, which in Julia's case was grammar.

Andy's speaking was very different to Julia's. He was able to use varied vocabulary and good grammar in speaking but he had great difficulties with pronunciation. Some of the sounds of Spanish were new to him; they did not exist in his mother tongue. Although Andy's writing was excellent, his spoken Spanish was hard to understand. The solution for him was to

focus more on pronunciation, another key ingredient of the spoken language.

From time to time, I find students whose biggest limitation is their small repertoire of vocabulary. But this is less common. Having a good range of words enables you to express yourself more clearly and is perhaps the key ingredient that people master most easily.

So, please pay attention to this powerful principle: to speak fluently and with precision you need to develop the three key ingredients of vocabulary, pronunciation, and grammar.

The number one key ingredient is vocabulary: we can't communicate at all without it. The second is pronunciation: we need to pronounce vocabulary reasonably well if we want to be understood. And third is grammar: a good command of grammar rules and structures helps us to understand and express ideas with accuracy. It is the icing on the cake!

What about you?

Which elements of Spanish do you find
easier to learn?

	Vocabulary	Pronunciation	Grammar
Very easy			
Easy			
Challenging			
Very challenging			

I would like mainly to improve:

Chapter 7
Taking advantage of supporting skills

Have you noticed the strong connection between listening and speaking skills? And have you realised that you need to do a good amount of listening to be good at speaking? When listening to Spanish, we get familiar with the sounds of the language, and the vocabulary and grammar used in conversations. All that is essential for becoming a good speaker of the language.

Other language skills are strongly interconnected too. For example, reading gives you exposure to a wide range of vocabulary and grammar structures. And as your range of vocabulary and grammar increases, so does your ability to read, listen, speak, and write.

Writing supports good speaking as well because, when writing, you usually have time to do things that improve your ability to express yourself such as:

• Selecting appropriate vocabulary and grammar for saying what you want to say.

• Using the dictionary to check the meaning of words you are not sure about.

• Checking the grammar and style of your message.

Writing is good preparation for good quality speaking. I see it happening with my students: if they write about a topic ahead of speaking about it, their oral communication will always be better. The quality of their speaking improves even more if they have also done reading and listening on the same topic.

Remember: listening, reading, speaking and writing are 'good friends'; they support each other. This is another powerful principle.

Skills gaps

There was a quiet knock on my office door. A student I did not recognise came in.

'Hi. My name is Yana. I'm struggling a bit with my Spanish course and my teacher said that you may be able to help with learning strategies.'

'OK, have a seat... What are you struggling with?'

'I'm finding the speaking part hard. The problem is that I can understand a lot more than I can say. I had the same problem when I did Spanish at school, and it's the same when I go on holiday with my family to southern Spain.'

Sometimes I come across students who, like Yana, are worried that they understand a lot more than they can speak or write in Spanish. And they assume that it's due to their not being good enough at speaking or writing, but that is not taking into account the skills gap that is inherent in all languages that we learn, mother tongue included.

The gap between receptive language skills (reading and listening) and productive language skills (writing and speaking) is natural for all of us. We easily understand the speeches of eloquent public speakers, but we may not find it easy to write or deliver similar speeches. The same goes for writing: understanding Mario Vargas Llosa novels without a problem does not mean that we can easily write literary works of this kind.

As a tourist in a Spanish-speaking country, we read signs, menus, and brochures, and we are surrounded by native speakers and hear all sorts of conversations. But many tourists get by, or even avoid having to speak much, and are hardly ever called on to write in Spanish during their trip. The bottom line is that they practise reading and listening skills a lot more than speaking and writing. This increases the gap between receptive and productive skills.

Some language teaching methods can also increase the gap between skills. For example, when I was studying English at school, we spent most of the time focusing on grammar, vocabulary, and reading. We hardly did any listening and speaking practice. So, on my first trips to the UK, I managed to understand texts like museum brochures and menus quite well, but I could not understand native speakers at all, not even when they used basic vocabulary while giving directions or telling me a phone number. Speaking was even harder: I could not even introduce myself without blushing! My speaking and listening skills were basically zero at that time, but I was reasonably comfortable reading and writing in real-life situations. The gap was so big that I thought I would never manage to get my speaking and listening up to speed. Fortunately, time proved me wrong.

Children who are brought up speaking Spanish at home but are living in a non-Spanish speaking country like the USA or the UK tend to experience the opposite. They develop strong listening and speaking skills because that is how they communicate with their parents at home from childhood. They are brought up on a diet of intensive listening and speaking but are hardly ever put

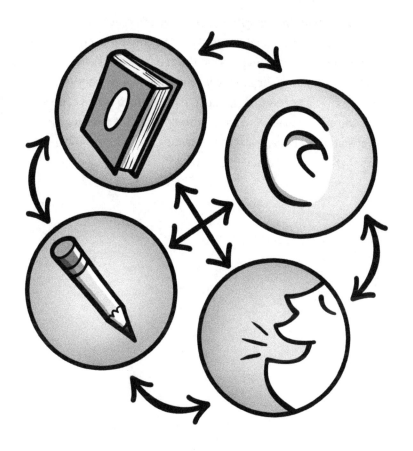

into a situation where they need to write or understand a written text. When they grow up, it is easy for them to speak fluently but many of them cannot write without making a lot of spelling mistakes.

There is nothing wrong with experiencing different levels of proficiency in different language skills. The situation only becomes problematic if you are finding that the gap between skills prevents you from communicating in the way you need to or want to. If that is the case, it is time for action. It is time to take a course, find a tutor or a coach, increase informal practice, or engage in other suitable language learning activities that improve the skills that you want to develop more.

What about you?

Before reading this chapter:

- Were you aware of the 'friendship' between reading, listening, writing, and speaking and how they strongly support each other?

- If yes, were you taking advantage of it? How?

POWERFUL STRATEGIES

Chapter 8
Expanding your vocabulary

I guess you do not need me to persuade you about the importance of learning a good range of Spanish words and phrases on a variety of topics. It's obvious that, without vocabulary, nothing can be expressed or understood. But since Spanish has thousands of words, the first big question is: *What is the best way to learn Spanish words?*

The answer is simple.

Vocabulary can be learnt in two ways:

1.   **By exposure, through reading and listening.** Whilst reading and listening, we become familiar with the meaning, spelling, use, and pronunciation of words and phrases.

2.   **By focused study.** We do that when we focus on memorising particular words and phrases using techniques such as written and verbal repetition, flashcards, or mind maps.

Both approaches complement each other. You get the best results for learning vocabulary by learning by both exposure and focused study.

And since there are thousands of words that can be learnt, the second big question is: *What vocabulary do I prioritise?*

I suggest you give priority to five categories that will help to speed up your learning and give you more confidence.

- **Cognates.** These are Spanish words similar or identical, in meaning and spelling, to words you know in other languages. If you already speak a language that originated in or has borrowed words from Latin, you will find many cognates in Spanish. For example, if you speak English, you will find it easy to remember Spanish words such as *aeropuerto*, *restaurante, hospital, hotel*, and *teléfono*. When learning cognates, keep in mind that there are a small number of false cognates: that is, words that have identical or similar spelling, but which mean something very different. For example, these are false cognates between English and Spanish: *mi pie* (does not mean *my pie* – it means *my foot*); *mi ropa* (does not mean *my rope* – it means *my clothes*); and *soy sensible* (does not mean *I am sensible* – it means *I am sensitive*). These are often called 'false friends'. It is always worth doing an initial check with a dictionary to make sure the cognate you are learning is correct.

- **Vocabulary formation rules.** Learn vocabulary rules that help to transfer large amounts of vocabulary between languages. For example, usually:

- Words ending in -tion in English change to -*ción* in Spanish (celebration–*celebración*, classification–*clasificación*)
- Words ending in -ity in English change to -*idad* in Spanish (tranquillity–*tranquilidad*, ability–*habilidad*)
- Words ending in -ous in English change to -*oso* or -*osa* in Spanish (famous–*famoso* or *famosa*, delicious–*delicioso* or *deliciosa*)
- Words ending in -ant in English change to -*ante* in Spanish (abundant–*abundante*, elegant–*elegante*)
- Adverbs ending in -ly in English change to -*mente* in Spanish (normally–*normalmente*, perfectly–*perfectamente*)
- Words ending in -ic in English change to -*ico* or -*ica* in Spanish (romantic–*romántico* or *romántica*, organic–*orgánico* or *orgánica*)

- **High-frequency vocabulary.** Well-designed courses and online resources already teach words and phrases that are frequently used. If you are studying by yourself, use study materials that teach high-frequency vocabulary and equip you well for real-life communication.

- **Collocations.** Another way of speeding up fluency in speaking and writing is learning collocations (words commonly used together). For example: *dar un paseo* (to go for a walk), *trabajo en equipo* (team work), *recursos naturales* (natural resources).

- **Expressions useful for you.** Make a point of learning vocabulary that you find particularly interesting or necessary for talking with people about your life.

What about you?

Are you paying attention to any of the five categories when learning vocabulary?

	√
Cognates	
Vocabulary formation rules	
High-frequency vocabulary	
Collocations	
Expressions useful for you	

Chapter 9
Three major benefits of grammar

'How many of you want to learn to speak very good Spanish?'
When I ask students this question, all of them raise their hands
without hesitation. But when I ask, 'How many of you are
looking forward to learning Spanish grammar?' the response
is significantly less enthusiastic; in many groups, only a few
students raise their hands. And when I ask them about their lack
of enthusiasm for grammar, they usually tell me that it is 'hard to
understand'. In some cases, students also believe that grammar is
not that important for speaking.

I can understand their resistance. I used to feel the same when
I was studying at school and at university. Although I enjoyed
studying Spanish grammar up to secondary education, I remember
finding it hard and boring in college. I did not see the point of
analysing the complex grammar structures in so much detail.
'What do I need this for?' I wondered many times.

Fortunately, nowadays foreign language courses usually focus on
teaching grammar for real-life communication. For example, if you
are learning how to talk about your weekly routine, you will be
taught the grammar that you need for that, such as reflexive verbs
(*levantarse*–to get up, *ducharse*–to have a shower, *acostarse*–to
go to bed), and periphrasis (*tener que* + infinitive–to have to do
something).

Current communicative teaching methods focus on teaching students the grammar they need for everyday communication. This practical approach is a major improvement in foreign language teaching. I hope you get to experience it.

But if you are one of those students who has some resistance to studying grammar, remember that learning key grammar rules and structures will improve your communication skills in three major ways:

- **Precision.** Good grammar will enable you to communicate with more accuracy. For example, as you probably know, different verb endings convey different meanings in Spanish. Saying, '*Trabajo en la universidad*' is not the same as saying, '*Trabaja en la universidad*'. In the first sentence I say that *I* work at the university, and in the second that *he or she* works at the university.

- **Creativity.** You will be able to express more ideas. For example, when you are able to use a variety of tenses, you can understand and talk about past, present, and future actions and events. You cannot do that if you only know the present tense.

- **Fluency.** You will develop more flow in speaking and writing. Once you have automatised word order, agreements, verb endings, and so on, you do not need to pause constantly to think about how to say what you want to communicate. You will understand others and express yourself with ease.

I am not suggesting that your grammar needs to be perfect. Errors are a natural part of learning, and we are still able to communicate effectively with less than perfect grammar. But it is worth remembering that good grammar will enable you to be more precise, creative, and fluent in Spanish. In the long term it pays off. It is worth the effort.

What about you?

- Had you thought before about how grammar impacts your precision, creativity and fluency when speaking and writing in Spanish?

- Can you find any other advantages to getting good at grammar?

Chapter 10
Prioritising and automatising your grammar

What grammar are you going to focus on? A good course will teach you grammar structures that are appropriate for your level. If you are studying by yourself, I recommend that you pay special attention to two areas:

- Spanish verbs. Learn the form (for example, endings, irregularities) and how to employ frequently used verbs. Verbs have a strong impact in communication because they appear in nearly every sentence, and they transmit important information: the action, who is doing it, and when.

- Grammar rules. It is worth memorising grammar rules that have few or no exceptions. One example is learning the Spanish grammar rule on word agreements (article, noun, adjective): there are no exceptions to this rule, and you will be using agreements constantly in Spanish.

Self-study materials for Spanish often include grammar summaries. They are very helpful for memorising important grammar points.

Automatising your grammar

Have you already noticed that memorising verbs and grammar rules does not automatically translate into using them easily in speaking or writing? Theoretical knowledge does not translate automatically into skill. That is the way it is. So, learning verb endings and grammar by heart is not enough.

To reach the goal of using grammar 'automatically', we need the two complementary approaches already mentioned in the chapter on vocabulary:

- Learning by exposure
- Learning by focused study

Learning by exposure is, as the word suggests, about exposing yourself to the grammar you want to learn through reading and listening to Spanish. Let's say that you want to learn to use the preterite and imperfect tenses. If that is the case, you need texts and audio-visual materials that expose you to those tenses many times. Biographies would be useful for this because accounts of people's lives use the preterite and the imperfect frequently.

Learning by focused study is especially important for grammar structures that you find complex.

Focused study can be done with three simple steps:

1. Select a grammar point
2. Study the form and uses
3. Memorise the form and uses

If you are learning the preterite and imperfect, you would:

1. Select the preterite and imperfect
2. Study the form of the regular and irregular verb endings and understand when to use the two tenses (similarities and differences)
3. Memorise the endings and uses through the practice of grammar drill activities, flashcards, and/or any other strategy that helps you with long-term memory retention

The combination of learning by exposure and learning by focused study will get you ready to use the two tenses with ease in speaking and writing.

When you start putting the tenses into practice, expect to make mistakes before you get good at it. The way to make sure you keep improving is by getting regular corrective and constructive feedback when you practise. That is the best way to avoid unconsciously repeating wrong forms and uses. Regular feedback gives you clarity on what you are automatising well and what you need to revise.

Online or printed grammar exercises where you can check the correct answers are great for getting instant corrective feedback. If you are practising with Spanish speakers, ask them to help you by correcting you. Constructive feedback from a good teacher or a coach will always take you further and faster in your progress.

What about you?

How have you approached learning
  grammar so far?

	Never/ rarely	Sometimes	Often	Very often
I have a positive attitude to grammar				
I practice learning grammar by exposure				
I practice learning grammar by focused study				

To improve my study of grammar, I could:

Chapter 11
Memorising better and for longer

Interest and *understanding* are two golden keys for remembering information. It makes sense, doesn't it? We pay more attention to things that we find interesting, and we remember things we understand well better than things we are confused about.

I see how these two keys work year after year with my students. For example, at the end of the academic year, students in beginners' classes remember and easily use vocabulary for food and activities that they like, such as: *patatas/papas fritas* (French fries), *pastel* (cake), *escuchar música* (to listen to music), *bailar* (to dance), *salir con mis amigos* (to go out with my friends), and *viajar* (to travel). I also notice that, when students invest enough time to understand how to form the verbs, they end up remembering them more easily and using the verb endings more accurately in speaking and writing. So, to memorise effectively, do your best to understand well the vocabulary and grammar that you are studying, and make it as interesting as possible so that you can remember it more easily.

This sequence helps long-term memorisation of vocabulary and grammatical structures:

1. Creating multiple associations
2. Using spaced study
3. Testing yourself

Let's look at the sequence through a real-life example, in this case the Spanish word *pasear*.

Step 1. Create multiple associations

Associate the word with things or language that you are already familiar with and which interest you such as:

- The translation. Check the meaning of *pasear* in the dictionary (to go for walk) and write it down.

- A picture. Associate the word *pasear* with a mental picture or a drawing of someone going for a walk.

- The sound. Listen to how the word *pasear* is pronounced, paying careful attention to the sounds and the stressed syllable. After listening well, repeat the word out loud.

- A collocation. Write down collocations with the word *pasear* such as: *pasear por el parque* (walk in the park), *pasear al perro* (walk the dog), *pasear con amigos* (walk with friends).

- Write a sentence or dialogue. Phrases and dialogues are usually more meaningful to us than single words. Write the word *pasear* in a sentence or a short dialogue which vibrates emotionally with you, for example: *me gusta mucho pasear por el parque* (I like walking in the park).

If you can think of humorous situations, all the better. Humour increases our degree of focus and the amount of attention we give to the thing we find funny.

Research into cognitive psychology and neuroscience has found that we learn new information better when we make meaningful mental connections, and that multisensory learning works best for long-term retention. That is why learning Spanish vocabulary and grammar is more effective when you hear how a word is pronounced, write it down, say it out loud, and associate the new word with pictures, colours, and graphics.

There are many strategies for creating multiple connections. You can write vocabulary and grammar in a notebook, use sticky notes, design flashcards, draw mind maps, use mnemonics, build a 'memory palace', and so on. I recommend that you pick one or two strategies that you find appealing, try them out for a month or so, and see how it goes. You may need to try several of them until you find what works best for you.

Step 2. Practise spaced study

Spaced study means that you review the vocabulary and grammar over a period of time instead of cramming it. Having gaps between revision gives the mind time to make connections between ideas and makes it easier to recall them later. It's better to space your revision periods. For example, if you have the Spanish lesson on Monday, start your revision of the new vocabulary and grammar two days after, on Wednesday, then again on Friday, and again the following Tuesday. You will need to play around with the periods of time that you leave between revisions until you find what works best for you.

Step 3. Test yourself

After doing revision, leave some space and then test yourself to check what you can remember without looking at your notes. Researchers have found that making the effort of trying to remember without any prompt strengthens the memory of what we are learning.

Testing can also be done in collaboration with other people. Perhaps you did this at school, when a friend or family member helped to test you before an exam.

If you decide to ask somebody to test you, choose someone who is positive and reasonably demanding so that you neither become discouraged nor miss out on the opportunity to receive proper feedback.

Acknowledging your progress is essential too. Sometimes it is not easy; we may not have been taught to celebrate our own progress in childhood. Yet most people blossom with positive reinforcement. Make it a habit to take notice of and enjoy the progress you are making.

What about you?

Are you practising any of the three steps for memorising vocabulary and grammar?

	√
1. Creating multiple associations	
2. Practising spaced study	
3. Testing yourself	

I would like to make improvements in:

Chapter 12
Improving your pronunciation

Achieving a good level of pronunciation in standard Spanish is simple for many students because most single sounds correspond with a single letter of the alphabet. After a short period of practice, it is possible to predict the pronunciation of most Spanish words you read, and also to spell words you hear, even if the words are completely new to you and you still don't understand their meaning.

Two more advantages of Spanish pronunciation:

- The language has only five vowel sounds (a, e, i, o, u), which are pronounced the same most of the time. The only exception is that the vowel 'u' is silent in some fixed-letter combinations.

- Word stress rules are simple and easy to memorise.

Because of this, many students of Spanish are able to reach a good level of pronunciation in a short period of time. It takes longer for students whose mother tongue does not have some of the Spanish sounds. If this is the case for you, don't worry. You just need more focused pronunciation practice.

The power of listen-read-and-repeat strategies

Over the years, I have seen students from all over the world improve their Spanish-speaking skills in a short period of time by using listen-read-and-repeat strategies.

The strategies are suitable for everyone and require only two types of resources: Spanish audios or videos for your level, plus their transcripts.

As always, their content should be interesting to you, and the language should neither be too easy nor too difficult for your level. It should stretch your speaking ability without making you feel that it is an impossible task.

The benefits of listen-read-and-repeat strategies go beyond improving pronunciation and boosting fluency. The intense focus on listening, reading, and repeating helps you to memorise words, collocations, and grammatical structures with less effort. Listen-read-and-repeat strategies are simple and highly effective because they can have a positive impact not only on your speaking but also on your writing, listening, and reading skills.

Listen-read-and-repeat strategies 1

This is the most basic set of strategies. Highly useful for beginners and lower intermediate students, it consists of a preparation phase and a three-step sequence.

Preparation phase. Before starting the pronunciation practice, do a quick check of the transcript and make sure you understand all the vocabulary. If necessary, check the meaning of the words you do not know in the dictionary. This will help you to avoid changing your focus to, 'What does this mean?' during what should be pronunciation practice. And then follow this sequence:

1. **Listen**. Just listen to the audio without looking at the transcript. Pay attention to the sounds of the language. Enjoy it. You are building a memory of the sounds of Spanish, and that is the basis of good pronunciation.

2. **Listen-read-and-repeat chunks.** Get the transcript in front of you and start the audio or video. Listen to a chunk of language whilst reading in silence from the transcript, then pause the playback, and then repeat it out loud. For example:

   - listen and read in silence: *¿Dónde vives?*

   - press pause

   - repeat out loud: *¿Dónde vives?*, imitating the pronunciation of the speaker as well as you can.

3. **Focus on challenging words.** Go over the transcript again, this time noticing the words that were not easy to pronounce. Practise them individually. Notice how, as you keep repeating them, the pronunciation becomes easier and more natural. Make an effort to pronounce the words well but do not get too obsessed about reaching perfect imitation, otherwise the practice becomes counterproductive.

And acknowledge your progress. Keep the experience as positive as you can. Enjoy it.

Listen-read-and-repeat strategies 2

This set of strategies works well for any level, from beginner up to advanced, and again, contains simple steps:

1. **Shadow the speaker.** Play the audio or video with the transcript in front of you. Repeat what is being said by the speaker as if you are their 'shadow'. Get as close as possible to the pace of the speaker's voice.

2. **Match the speaker.** Now do your best to become one with the speaker's voice, whilst reading the transcript. Have fun with it.

3. **Record yourself.** Read out loud the transcript you have been practising in steps 1 and 2. Record yourself and then listen to the recording. Notice the improvements, and the sounds or words that may need further practice. Enjoy and be patient with it: developing good pronunciation is an ongoing process.

Singing along

I recommend you use listen-read-and-repeat strategies with Spanish songs too. In fact, if you think about it, when we listen to songs we like, we naturally use the listen-read-and-repeat strategies I have just explained. We often listen to a song we like, read the lyrics, and then we keep singing along until finally we can sing the song at the same pace as the singer.

Creating a playlist with Spanish music you like and singing along from time to time can help you to improve your Spanish. It is a fun and easy informal language learning practice.

More strategies

Start with single words. Get into the habit of practising pronunciation when checking single words in an audio dictionary. After looking at the meaning of a word, click on the audio, listen, and repeat the word out loud. Do a few drills on the spot. It pays off. You are building good pronunciation one word at a time.

Work on challenging words. Make the pronunciation of challenging words easier by following three simple steps. Let's imagine that you want to pronounce a word like *electrodoméstico* (household appliance).

1. **Spot the stressed syllable.** Listen to how the word is pronounced in the audio dictionary and spot the strongest syllable: *electrodoMÉStico*.

2. **Chunk the word.** Break it into small chunks and pronounce each one separately: *elec-trodo-MÉS-tico*. Words that initially look daunting become manageable if you break them down and pronounce the chunks one at a time.

3. **Join the chunks.** Make the chunks progressively longer and say them out loud until you can pronounce the entire word without pausing: *elec-trodo-MÉS-tico > electrodo-MÉStico > electrodoMÉStico*.

Once you have completed the three steps, listen to the audio again. Are you getting closer to the audio dictionary pronunciation? If you still don't find it easy to pronounce the word, ask yourself whether it is down to one or more of these reasons:

- Insufficient listening. You have not listened to how the word sounds enough times, so you have not yet built a good memory of the sounds and stressed syllable. Solution: More listening repetitions.

- Unfamiliar sounds. The word contains sounds that are still not easy for you to pronounce. Solution: Patience and more focused practice.

- Lack of focus. Your mind is wandering and busy thinking about other things. Solution: Bring full attention to the pronunciation practice activity.

Practise the three stress rules. They tell you how to spot the stressed syllable in any Spanish word.

Rule 1. If a word ends in 'n', 's', or a vowel (a, e, i, o, u), the stress goes onto the penultimate syllable, for example: *CaRAcas, eXAmen, aMIgo, cerVEza, fiESta.*

Rule 2. If a word ends in consonants other than 'n' and 's', the stress goes onto the last syllable, for example: *MaDRID, espaÑOL, amisTAD.*

Rule 3. In words that do not follow rules 1 and 2, the stressed syllable will be indicated with a written accent, for example: *PortuGUÉS, inGLÉS, MÉxico, BogoTÁ.*

Get a pronunciation app. If you want to do intensive pronunciation work with specific sounds of Spanish, you could get a pronunciation app that shows how to position the speech organs and gives you varied multimedia activities for practising.

What about you?

Check which of the pronunciation strategies mentioned in this chapter you are already using and identify those you could now incorporate into your practice.

	√
Doing listen-read-and-repeat exercises with audios/ videos	
Singing along to Spanish music	
Practising the pronunciation of words when checking their meaning in the dictionary	
Doing focused practice on words that are challenging to pronounce	
Practising the three stress rules	
Practising pronunciation with an app	

Chapter 13
Mastering flashcard design

I was marking Iwona's essays and, as on previous occasions, was impressed by the variety of vocabulary she had used. Her essays were amongst the best I had seen in many years of teaching Spanish. 'What do you do to produce so much good vocabulary, Iwona?' I asked when returning her essay.

'Oh, I use flashcards,' she replied.

'How? What kind of flashcards?'

'I make flashcards of the vocabulary I want to learn after each Spanish lesson. Then I revise them twice before I go to the next lesson. I usually revise on Wednesdays and Thursdays while I'm at the till of the gift shop where I work. Those days are quiet – there are times when there's nobody around. I spend about ten minutes reviewing the cards – it takes very little time. I do it because I don't like checking the dictionary constantly when I'm writing. I enjoy writing more when I already know the vocabulary.'

Felicity, another student, was attending the same Spanish class as Iwona, but she was struggling to keep up with the course. She was a very motivated student, one of the most motivated in her class, but Spanish was a challenging subject for her. This was not surprising to me considering that she had just arrived in the UK from a foreign country to study a demanding university course with fairly basic English. On top of all that, she also needed to work at her part-time job. No wonder she often looked exhausted in class.

One day close to the exam, as we were about to start doing revision for the test, Felicity walked through the door looking unusually confident. I was impressed by her speaking performance during the class – it was the best I had heard from her since the beginning of the year. At the end of the lesson, I asked how she had managed to catch up so quickly and so well. She smiled back, pulled out a stack of bright yellow and green flashcards from her bag, and spread them on the table. I could see flashcards that had been nicely crafted with careful handwriting and small sketches. She went on to explain how she had decided to try flashcards after a class discussion about language learning strategies. 'It was easy and fun to do revision with the cards, Maria! It was fun making them, too,' she said.

The stories of Iwona and Felicity are just two examples of the many positive experiences that my students have reported using flashcards. They find them convenient for revision-on-the-go since they can carry the electronic ones on their mobile or the printed ones in a pocket or handbag. And they often say that flashcards help them to memorise more effectively than any other strategy they have used.

I often see big improvements in performance and self-confidence once students start using flashcards for revision. I highly recommend you try them out if you are not using them already.

Strategies for designing your flashcards

There are many ways to design flashcards. It is a creative activity: you can play around with the content, format and illustrations. For example, you could use flashcards for learning words, collocations, questions and answers, rules, grammar structures, or short lists of verb endings. You also have the choice of electronic or paper flashcards. Flashcard apps are convenient for language learning since they include audio, a voice recorder, vocabulary games, and a spaced repetition system. They are very popular nowadays, but I still find students who use paper flashcards, and others who often combine formats, both electronic and paper.

When you create flashcards, I suggest you apply four strategies that can help you remember new vocabulary and grammar better.

- **Add images.** There is evidence from research studies that we remember information much more easily when it is supported by relevant visuals. So, when creating the flashcards, include pictures or drawings associated with the vocabulary and grammar you are learning.

- **Use colour-coding systems.** For example: stick to using one colour for feminine nouns and a different colour for masculine nouns; and highlight in red irregularities in verb conjugations. I am very fond of colour coding: it requires little effort and can give big returns. I discovered its power when I introduced colour coding in my Spanish grammar PowerPoint presentations. After doing that, I noticed that my students used verbs and word agreements with more accuracy, and the percentage of errors in agreements came down dramatically in the speaking test. It was remarkable to see such a dramatic improvement in the students' spoken grammar as a result of using colour coding in the lessons.

- **Use different letter formatting.** The reason for using different letter formatting is the same as for colour coding: it directs our attention to differences and helps to contrast. This is very useful when learning Spanish verbs. For example, if you write the verb endings in capital letters and the roots in lower case, you can easily see the contrast between both parts of the verb. And using capital letters for the ending will draw your attention to them. You could also put the endings in bold to reinforce the contrast.

Here is an example of a flashcard for learning the singular forms of the regular verbs in the present tense in Peninsular Spanish:

habl-O	habl-AMOS
habl-AS	habl-ÁIS
habl-A	habl-AN

- **Group the cards by topic.** Grouping language by topic such as free time activities, social media issues, job application, and regular past tenses enhances comprehension and memorisation of the language.

Once your flashcards are ready, you simply need to apply the spaced study and testing yourself strategies discussed in Chapter 11: Memorising better and for longer.

What about you?

- Are you already using electronic or paper flashcards for learning vocabulary and grammar?

- If not, would you like to start designing them?

- If you already use them, how can you make the design more effective?

Chapter 14
Selecting your learning resources

Using good Spanish learning resources is very important for your studies, especially if you are not living in a place where you get to hear, read, speak and write Spanish regularly.

I recommend you build your own resources kit with two types of materials: educational and authentic.

Educational resources

Educational resources are those specifically designed for learning purposes. They are excellent for understanding how the language works and for doing focused practice.

My ideal educational resources kit includes:

- A multimedia self-study course. It helps you to create a solid foundation of the language.

- An online dictionary. Obviously essential, and freely available on the internet with audio input, which is a great feature for getting good at pronunciation.

- A grammar book or app/website. I recommend one that gives clear theoretical grammar explanations, examples of usage, and grammar exercises along with the answers.

- A vocabulary book or app/website. One that introduces you to new vocabulary and provides exercises with answers. Ideally with relevant illustrations.

- Graded readers. These are an excellent resource for 'flooding' your brain with interesting and comprehensible Spanish input.

Authentic resources

Authentic resources are the perfect complement to educational resources because they give you the opportunity to listen to and read real-life language produced by native speakers.

You have a wide range of authentic materials for free or at very low cost to choose from on the internet. These include: information brochures, transport timetables, shop catalogues, comics, cartoons, receipts, announcements, advertisements, newspapers, magazines, books, movies, songs, radio and TV programmes, soap operas, songs, computer games, video clips, and social media messages.

When selecting resources, especially authentic resources, remember that you do not need to understand every single word to benefit from them. However, the language should not be too challenging; if you can barely understand anything, you will learn very little and lose confidence. At the same time, resources should not be too easy to understand if you want to make good progress. The language should stretch you but you should still feel that you can handle it without constantly checking the dictionary.

What about you?

Are you using any of these educational and authentic resources?

	√
Multimedia self-study course	
Online dictionary with audio input	
Grammar book / app / website with activities	
Vocabulary book / app / website with activities	
Graded readers	
Songs	
Films	
TV programmes	
Radio programmes	
Podcasts	

I would like to start using these resources:

Chapter 15
Getting good professional help

I recommend to students to keep taking good Spanish courses regardless of their level of proficiency – beginner, intermediate, or advanced. A good course offers well-designed topics, a variety of learning activities and materials, and a well-trained teacher. It gives many opportunities for focus and intense practice of the four language skills (speaking, listening, reading, writing), vocabulary, pronunciation, and grammar. This kind of practice helps students to express themselves and understand other people with precision in spoken and written Spanish.

Learning a language is like doing a jigsaw puzzle of a large landscape. Completing the landscape gets easier when you start by identifying and assembling a few pieces of the tree, a few of the river, a few of the mountain, and then, bit by bit, you enlarge the clusters until the full landscape emerges. A similar process takes place in a good language course: you are helped to identify key elements of vocabulary, pronunciation and grammar, to put these together, and then to expand those clusters until the fuller 'landscape' of the language emerges.

I also recommend being proactive in finding Spanish teachers or coaches who are passionate about teaching, who have creative and effective ways of facilitating learning, and who believe in the students' ability to do well. Good professionals also expect good work from students and provide constructive feedback to help them understand areas of progress and areas that require more attention. Good professionals make it possible for students to achieve results that go well beyond what they initially thought possible.

A solid foundation

I opened my inbox and found an email from Jo, a student I had taught the previous year.

```
Hola María,
Just wondering whether to retake the Spanish
beginners' course I did last year or whether to
enrol in the next level. Would it be possible
to do the beginners' course again? I would like
to carry on with Spanish, but I know that my
basic Spanish is not very good; I would feel
more comfortable with starting the year again.
What do you think?
```

It was nice to hear from Jo again. She had gone through a rough year. Although she had strong motivation to learn Spanish, difficult family circumstances led to her missing many lessons and struggling to keep up with her studies. I was glad to know that she was back and wanted to carry on studying.

Jo was willing to retake her beginners' course. Not many people are willing to do that. Retaking is often considered a sign of failure, while speeding forward to higher levels is considered a sign of success. But Jo was ready to slow down in order to consolidate a good basic level of Spanish, and I supported her in that because I strongly believe that, in the medium and long term, a solid foundation saves students a lot of time, struggle and stress. A solid foundation prevents gaps in knowledge and skills, prevents repeated errors, and helps students to experience more ease and confidence when communicating in Spanish from the start. That is why, sometimes, retaking a course, especially at the lower levels, is the smartest thing to do.

What about you?

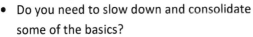

If you have already started learning Spanish:

- Have you acquired a solid foundation in the language?

- Do you need to slow down and consolidate some of the basics?

- What would you like to strengthen at a basic level, if anything?

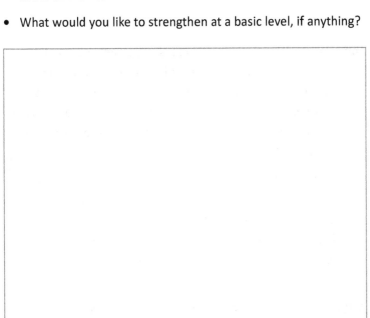

If you know that, for example, you have significant gaps in grammar, do try to identify the topics that you need to consolidate. Sometimes, it is as simple as working on a topic with a good grammar activity book. In other cases, it may be better to get some private lessons to fill in the gaps. Once you do it, you will feel more confident and will be able to express yourself better in Spanish. Building a solid base is worth the effort.

Chapter 16
Diving into immersion

Bob was travelling to Spain for the first time knowing very little Spanish. He was going for a weekend to Barcelona with some friends. They were in adventure mode and had decided not to book hotel rooms in advance. 'We'll just go with the flow and look for places to stay once we arrive,' he told me before leaving. And so they went.

On his return, when I asked about his trip, his face lit up. 'We had a great time – loved Barcelona, the food, the night life, the weather. Gaudi's architecture is amazing. We even saw FC Barcelona play at the Nou Camp. It's one of the best trips I've ever done! We also made some Spanish friends at the match. I'm planning to go back this summer to see them.'

'Did you manage to practise some Spanish?' I asked.

He smiled. 'Well, I was surprised how much the basic Spanish we learned in class helped me to communicate with people and get things done. Like the first night, when we went to a café. We were having dinner and watching a football match on the TV, and I started chatting to a Spanish man on the next table. His English was as basic as my Spanish, so we kept talking and switching between both languages. I managed to understand quite a lot of what he was telling me in Spanish, and we made a good connection. Later on, he helped us to find accommodation in a hotel nearby.'

Bob's attitude in class was transformed by his short visit to Barcelona. Before the trip, he had often been distracted in class, more interested in socialising with his classmates than in learning Spanish. But the trip changed him. He paid a lot more attention in the lessons and was happier and more productive in all the class activities. His transformation showed in his academic results: by the end of the course, he was doing really well in all the language skills, and he passed the Spanish exams comfortably.

Full immersion in a Spanish-speaking country can help you to greatly expand your language repertoire. Routine activities such as shopping, ordering food, arranging outings, or talking about your plans with native speakers are ideal situations for intense language practice. A trip to a grocery store easily becomes a lesson on food, instructions, and numbers – you may be reading food labels, asking the shop assistant where to find certain products, reading the product names on your receipt, and hearing the cashier telling you the total of your bill.

This kind of intense and contextualised reading, speaking, and listening facilitates smooth acquisition and long-term retention of productive and receptive vocabulary. Receptive vocabulary is all the words and phrases you understand when you read or hear them, even if you cannot use them when you speak or write. Productive vocabulary is all the words and phrases you understand and that you are able to use when you speak and write. Expanding both types of vocabulary is essential for having good communication skills.

Full immersion also provides opportunities for improving fluency and our understanding of cross-cultural values. On this note, I remember Paul, one of my Spanish intermediate students, talking about his summer language exchange in Salamanca. He told me how Álvaro, his exchange partner, had often taken him to his family and friends' homes for dinner so that he could mix with native speakers and experience more of the local gastronomy. Paul described those dinners as amongst the most intense learning experiences of both language and culture that he had ever had.

'Conversations moved swiftly from one topic to another: travel experiences, politics, local gossip, traditions, finances, family plans, and many others. It was hard work because, when they chat, they take turns very fast, but I made an effort to take part in the conversations. I noticed that my fluency in Spanish improved after the dinners, and I got more confident about talking with native speakers. I also realised that their family ties are very strong. I lost count of the number of Álvaro's cousins I met and the number of occasions we were invited to stay or eat at his relatives' homes. Even when we went sightseeing to other cities, like Segovia, Álvaro would call them, and they would invite us to their home for lunch. I had never experienced anything like that before.'

Diving deep into Spanish language and culture transformed Paul's Spanish and expanded his cross-cultural understanding. The same happens to many students who spend a period of time immersed in a Spanish-speaking country.

With Spanish you are spoiled for choice since you have many Spanish-speaking countries to choose from. Bear in mind, though, that regional languages, in some cases quite different from standard Spanish, are widely spoken in certain regions: Catalán or Gallego are examples. So you may want to do some research on what languages or dialects you will encounter before travelling.

More options

There are more options that offer different levels of immersion in Spanish language and culture. For example, there are online language exchange sites where you can arrange face-to-face or online language exchanges. Some sites integrate access to free and premium multimedia materials with access to online tutors and forums where you can interact with native speakers. They offer a virtual meeting environment to learn Spanish with people who are enthusiastic about foreign languages, travelling, and discovering new cultures.

Other smart options are social events organised by Spanish clubs. Online networking sites such as meetup.com are good places to find clubs where Spanish native speakers and students get together for language exchanges, watching films, discussing books, salsa dancing, eating out, and so on. When my students attend those kinds of events, they often comment on the friendly atmosphere and end up making friends.
I also notice great improvements in their speaking skills and self-confidence.

Finally, there are some classic, low cost, and convenient options for immersing yourself in Spanish language and culture: books, music, TV, YouTube, radio programmes, movies. I have already recommended their use in Chapters 5 and 12, when discussing the importance of their role in learning. Nowadays, we do not have to travel anywhere to access a wide range of music, movies, programmes and books – we can get them at reasonable prices or for free on our mobiles, tablets, or PCs. Having so much choice available means that you are sure to find something that interests you. Once you have the resources, you could:

- **Read for pleasure.** Just as you do in your mother tongue, choose stories you like with a level of Spanish comprehensible to you. The language should be slightly above your current level so that it stretches your ability, but not so difficult that you have to constantly check the dictionary – unless, of course, you enjoy doing word by word translations!

- **Listen to songs.** Find Spanish songs that you like and listen to them. Remember that, even if you do not understand a lot of the lyrics, you will become familiar with the sounds of the language, and some vocabulary will stick in your mind. Of course, to imitate the sounds of any foreign language well, you first need to hear them.

- **Listen and sing.** As I mentioned earlier on in the book, listening and singing to songs is an informal and enjoyable way of improving your pronunciation, listening skills, and vocabulary.

- **Listen to radio and podcasts.** This is an ideal activity at a higher intermediate and advanced level, and it is simple to set up. There is a wide range of programmes on the internet. What do you prefer? Comedy? News? Entertainment? Educational programmes? Listening to the programmes will refine your listening skills and teach you vocabulary for discussing a variety of topics.

- **Watch movies.** I guess that you do not need much encouragement for this. Watching movies is a popular activity for people who are interested in learning foreign languages. And the great thing is that, besides being pleasurable, watching movies has three more major benefits. First, the characters show how to use Spanish in real-life environments: home, workplace, public spaces, and so on. Also, research shows that the association between spoken words and images in audio-visual materials helps us to better understand the meaning of words and store them in our long-term memory. And finally, you get to learn a lot about the culture of Spanish-speaking countries because most movies give information and discuss opinions on current affairs, politics, history, art, science, and so on.

A word of caution: use subtitles wisely. There is not much point in watching movies in Spanish if you can hardly understand what is being said. In that case, it is better to turn on the subtitles of your mother tongue or another language you speak very well. Remember that, to learn a foreign language, first, we need to be able to understand it. So only turn off the mother tongue subtitles or use Spanish subtitles once you can understand what is being said quite well. Once you get to this point, turning on the Spanish subtitles is a great way to learn new vocabulary because you are listening to words, seeing the context in which they are used, and reading their spelling all at the same time. You are creating multiple associations that lead to a deeper learning of new words and phrases. Watching movies this way can increase your vocabulary exponentially.

What about you?

- Have you experienced full immersion in Spanish?

- Are you considering spending a period of time in a Spanish-speaking country?

- Is there any Spanish-speaking country you feel drawn to visit?

- Are you using any other immersion options? Are there any you may want to try?

	√
Online language exchanges	
Spanish cultural and social clubs	
Listening to radio or podcasts	
Listening to songs	
Reading for pleasure	
Watching movies or TV programmes	

Chapter 17
Checking for self-limiting beliefs

Self-doubt and self-limiting beliefs often kick in during the process of learning. They are frequently rooted in negative reinforcements received in childhood from teachers, family members, or other people in authority. We end up believing we are not good at grammar, not good at speaking, and so on. We believe that this is the truth and things will stay like that forever. We carry around those beliefs unconsciously without asking ourselves: Are they true?

I remember a self-development workshop at which we discussed this topic in depth and experimented with powerful processes to let go of self-limiting beliefs. The workshop leader asked us to get into groups of four to discuss the self-limiting beliefs that we wished to overcome. Jenny, one of the participants in my group, volunteered to start sharing.

'I would like to get rid of the belief that I am not good at learning foreign languages. I was not good at languages at school. My German teacher always said that my grammar was poor. I barely managed to pass the compulsory exams, and then forgot all about learning foreign languages until recently. But my partner and I are planning to take a sabbatical to travel around the world next year, and we'd like to start with a long trip across Latin America. I would love to learn some Spanish before the trip to be able to talk and mix with the locals and to get closer to their culture. My local adult education college runs Spanish evening courses, but I keep putting off enrolling. I'm not sure whether I'll do well.'

The rest of the group began to ask questions.

'What made you think that you weren't good at learning languages when you were at school?' I asked.

'I didn't understand grammar – I found it hard. My teacher said many times that my grammar was poor. At one point, I just gave up on the language and concentrated on passing the exams. I passed with a very low mark.'

'What makes you think it will be the same now?' someone else asked her.

'I'm a lot more motivated than I was at school, particularly because of our trip to Latin America, but I haven't learned more grammar since I left school. I'm not sure whether I can do any better now.'

After a few more questions and comments from the group, Jenny started looking more relaxed.

Jenny's story remained in my head. I could connect very well with her frustration and lack of confidence. I had experienced similar emotions while learning English as a foreign language. At one point, when I was at intermediate level, I remember thinking that I had reached the ceiling of my capacity. I was sure that my pronunciation, vocabulary, and grammar were never going to get better. To say that it was frustrating would be an understatement. Fortunately, I did not give up. I kept going and broke the glass ceiling, reaching an advanced level of English.

My motivation to learn was stronger than my fears. I wanted to live and work in the UK and other English-speaking environments without experiencing limitations when communicating in English. I am quite talkative when it comes to things that I care about, and I could not settle for not being able to participate fully in conversations that mattered to me. Strong motivation was on my side. Also, while teaching and researching the way we learn foreign languages, I got to understand that people who are considered good at languages apply principles and strategies which can be easily replicated. This realisation is one of the most empowering insights of my education.

Now that I have taught Spanish for so many years, to so many students, of so many nationalities, I can see that anybody can overcome learning challenges when they have strong motivation and good professional support and are ready to put in the necessary work. They always succeed. There is no glass ceiling that cannot be broken. There is no limit! Remember that.

What about you?

Do you have any self-limiting beliefs around your ability to learn Spanish?

If you have self-limiting beliefs, I suggest you discuss them with someone who can help you to let them go. Good teachers and coaches are ideal for that. You may also find people in your family or circle of friends who are able to help you to turn limiting beliefs around. The more you get to feel the 'I can do it', the easier and happier your language learning experience will be.

Chapter 18
Taking action

The principles and strategies discussed in this book bring about deep changes and long-lasting results when you apply them. Knowledge can give you clarity about the process of language learning, but you must apply the knowledge to get results. Remember: clarity is power, action brings results.

The following steps will help you to focus and to move forward whether you are a complete beginner or are taking your Spanish up to a higher level. The steps are both simple and powerful.

1. Clarify your motivation. Think about why you are learning Spanish. Review the exercise you did in Chapter 1: What motivates you? on listing the reasons why you want to learn Spanish.

2. Set your Spanish learning goals. If you have not done so yet, give yourself some time to write down your goals considering these two important points:

- Learning goals are more powerful when they are connected to a wider vision like wanting to learn more about other cultures, wanting to connect with new relatives and friends, wanting to open up to better professional opportunities, or wanting to offer good quality customer service to Spanish-speaking clients.

- Learning goals give you a clear destination, and help you to develop good strategies, acknowledge your successes, and become aware of the skills or elements of the language that require more work.

3. Experiment with new language learning strategies. Keep using the strategies that are already working well for you and try out new ones. Select new strategies that appeal to you; apply and play with them for a while, notice changes and results. Enjoy your progress and make adjustments to keep the learning experience positive. Increasing your range of strategies increases your learning power.

Keep in mind the powerful principles presented in Part Two of the book:

- Combine formal and informal learning activities. Both approaches will help you to become fluent and accurate in Spanish.

- Listen to and read interesting and understandable Spanish regularly. The more you do that, the easier you will find it to speak and write.

- Work on vocabulary, pronunciation and grammar, since those are the key elements of language skills.

- Practise the four skills (listening, reading, writing and speaking) because each one of them supports the development of the others.

Your three-step Spanish learning action plan:

1. I choose to learn Spanish because:

| |
| |

2. My Spanish learning goals are:

| |
| |

3. I am going to explore these strategies:

```

```

We are coming to the end of the book. My final piece of advice
to you is, wherever possible, enrol in a regular class, conversation
club, language exchange or similar face-to-face or online
community where you can interact with other learners or native
Spanish speakers. Group support can provide great intellectual
stimulation, opportunities to practise listening and speaking skills,
encouragement, and useful resources.

For additional information or coaching support on the language
learning principles and strategies presented in this book, you can
contact me through www.forlearningspanish.com

With best wishes for your Spanish learning experience.

María Blanco

Acknowledgments

I am very grateful to a long list of friends, family members, students, colleagues and book production professionals for the inspiration and support in the writing of the first and revised editions of this book:

To the students and teacher trainees who have attended my lessons, workshops and coaching sessions. Their positive feedback motivates me to carry on researching, coaching and writing on this topic. Special thanks to Elmira and Madalina for participating enthusiastically in the training sessions and research projects.

To my parents, Jorge and Teresa, and my family for giving me so many educational opportunities and being such a good example of how much can be achieved with discipline.

To my meditation teacher, Ratu Bagus, and our international community for the daily dose of happy vibes and extraordinary support that make "the impossible become possible".

To my close friends for the solid network of support and motivation. Special thanks to Vijay and Lynne for the discussions and technical and editing support from day one, and to Libu for her artistic input on the book cover.

To my colleagues at the University of Westminster and other educational institutions with whom I interact regularly. Thank you for the stimulating conversations, teamwork and shared passion for good quality language teaching and learning.

To Rachel Paling for her Neurolanguage Coaching© course. It was highly enjoyable and took my understanding of language learning to a deeper level.

Finally, deep gratitude to Isabel, Dawn, Scott, Martha and Susan for the great professional work and easy-going communication in the processes of managing, editing, illustrating, typesetting and copyediting the book. Thank you for making the dream come true.

About the Author

MARÍA BLANCO is a Spanish Language Teacher, Neurolanguage Coach®, language learning strategies specialist and Senior Lecturer in Spanish in the University of Westminster.

She has worked designing, teaching and assessing Spanish courses since 1996 and delivers coaching, talks and workshops on language learning strategies for students and teachers in the UK and Europe. She has also worked as Spanish Development Editor for Hodder and Stoughton in the Foreign Language Graded Reader Series.

At *For LEARNING SPANISH,* she designs and leads workshops and coaching sessions that enable students and teachers to learn simple and powerful language learning principles and strategies. The workshops and coaching sessions help learners of Spanish to take charge, speed up their learning, feel more empowered and confident, and experience more creativity and playfulness in their language learning.

María studied her BA (Hons) in Education at the Universidad Pontificia de Salamanca (Spain), and completed an MA in Modern Languages in Education at the University College of London Institute of Education. She is a Neurolanguage Coach® certified by

Efficient Language Coaching and accredited by the International Coaching Federation. She is also a certified EUROLTA Teacher Trainer, International House Spanish Language Teacher and Online Tutor, and Fellow of the Higher Education Academy.

For information about María's coaching and workshops on language learning strategies go to www.forlearningspanish.com.

First published in 2021
by Hikari Press, London
www.hikaripress.co.uk

© María Blanco 2021

ISBN: 978-1-8384146-0-3

Revised edition of
Smart Ways for Learning Spanish, 2017

Distributed in the UK by
Combined Book Services Limited
Paddock Wood
Tonbridge
Kent TN12 6UU
www.combook.co.uk

British Library Cataloguing-in-Publication-Data.
A catalogue record of the book is available
from the British Library.

Illustrations by Scott DuBar
Edited by Dawn Stoddart and Lynne Kay
Designed in Calibri by Libanus Press Ltd

CPSIA information can be obtained
at www.ICGtesting.com
Printed in the USA
BVHW090830111021
618671BV00010B/416